The Communication Works

# Book 1:
# Self Confidence &
# Assertiveness

**Caroline Hopkins**

THE
COMMUNICATION
**WORKS**

*Also by Caroline Hopkins*

Help! I've Got A Presentation Coming Up
The Communication Works Book 2: Empathy & Negotiation Skills
The Communication Works Book 3: Networking & Influence Skills

First Printing: 2018
ISBN 978-0-244-66856-3

**Hopkins & Ball Ltd**
**The Innovation Centre, Sci-Tech Daresbury**
**Warrington, Cheshire WA4 4FS**
**www.hopkinsandball.com**

Ordering Information:
Special discounts are available on quantity purchases by corporations, associations, educators, and others. For details, contact the publisher at the above listed address.

# CONTENTS

# INTRODUCTION

# Introduction

How often have you come away from a situation feeling frustrated that you said too little or too much?

As someone who has spent much of my life having to apologise after the event, or berate myself that I didn't speak up when I had the chance, I wanted to find ways to manage my response so I felt more in control and able to express myself without self-recrimination or resentment.

I learnt early on that assertive communication is directly linked to our self-communication - our emotional response and our inner voice - so that we feel comfortable to express ourselves, our thoughts and feelings, without fear or guilt that we have overwhelmed others or underwhelmed ourselves by not speaking up when we had the chance.

There are 3 key steps to having greater mastery of your self-communication: Awareness of what is currently happening when you try to assert yourself, Strategies to manage your thoughts/feelings/actions in situations where you would like to improve your communication; and Practice – so that these new habits of responding to people and situations become second nature.

This book draws on several areas of behavioural psychology to help you become more assertive and self-confident in handling other people, tricky situations and managing your own emotions more effectively – so that you can, as the saying goes... Say What You Mean, Without Saying It Mean'.

# "Go For It!"

your inner voice
(when it feels ready)

# Chapter 1:

# HOW TO BE MORE CONFIDENT

"A ship in a harbour is safe, but that is not what ships are built for"

J. A. Shedd

# Chapter 1: How To Be More Confident

## The TEA Model

What makes a confident person... or a person confident?

When I ask this question in workshops, people will come up with words like
*Presence, charisma, knowledge, experience, self-belief, calmness, inner strength, motivation, determination, happy in their skin...*

All of these are signs of confidence in a person - and you will probably have your own list of features that you would ascribe to confident people – but you will notice these attributes will cluster into 3 key areas: confident people have confident THOUGHTS (their beliefs and self-talk reinforce why they can do something); they have confident EMOTIONS (they feel OK about things, they can overcome fear and manage negative emotions) and they ACT with confidence (they get on an do things, they look and sound confident).

This happy threesome: Thoughts – Emotions – Action, known as the TEA-Model, is a useful framework in managing your confidence.

It works as a model because the three areas are inter-dependent; each area will influence the other two areas. You can boost or deflate your confidence through the interaction of your Thoughts, Emotions and Actions by leading with the area you find easiest to control.

Having more confident thoughts affects how you feel and act; acting confidently impacts on your thoughts and emotions; get into a confident emotional state and your thoughts and actions will be led by your mood.

The first step is being aware of what you are currently doing to manage your confidence in each area, so you can identify and apply different strategies to get better results.

The three chapters which follow will help you to do just that: to explore what you can do to have the kind of Thoughts, Emotions and Actions that will create more confidence in yourself, your outlook and your experiences.

**'If you always do what you've always done,
You'll always get what you always got.'**

NLP Presupposition

# Chapter 2:

# CHALLENGING NEGATIVE THINKING

# "Whether you think you can, or think you can't… you're right"

## Henry Ford

# Chapter 2: Challenging Negative Thinking

In this chapter we will cover how you can get into the habit of having more positive THOUGHTS to become more self-confident.

What do you think all these people have in common?

>Tom Hanks
>Neil Gaiman
>John Green
>Tommy Cooper
>Sheryl Sandberg
>US Supreme Court justice, Sonia Sotomayor
>Emma Watson
>Maya Angelou

They all suffer from the 'Imposter Syndrome', a concept that was first coined in 1978 by psychologists Pauline Clance and Suzanne Imes to describe people with 'an inability to internalize their accomplishments and a persistent fear of being exposed as a fraud'.

Despite external evidence of their competence, sufferers of the Imposter Syndrome believe that they *are* frauds and do not deserve the success they have achieved. Proof of success is dismissed as luck, timing, or as a result of deceiving others into thinking they are more intelligent and competent than they really are.

Clance later said it would have been better to call it the 'Imposter Experience' because "it's not a syndrome or a complex or a mental illness, it's something almost everyone experiences at some time".

The Imposter Syndrome is perfectly summed up by Lou Solomon, who in her TED talk (you can find her talk at www.ted.com) describes the imposter syndrome as "having a crappy best friend in your head who says mean things to you".

Most people will experience the imposter syndrome at times in their lives, but some people live with it: they have made it into a habit and engage in an ongoing negative commentary to reinforce their feelings of self-doubt. Like any habit it can be changed, but you need the three-part harmony of 'awareness, intention and action' to break the pattern.

Maya Angelou, the author, poet and Nobel Laureate, expressed her 'imposter' thoughts like this:

*"I have written 11 books, but each time I think, 'Uh oh, they're going to find out now. I've run a game on everybody, and they're going to find me out."*

Meryl Streep, who holds the record for the most Oscar nominations of any actor, is quoted as saying *"Why would anyone want to see me again in a movie? And I don't know how to act anyway so why am I doing this?"*

Ironically, Jodie Foster, another imposter syndrome sufferer, is quoted as saying: *'When I won the Oscar, I thought it was a fluke. I thought everybody would find out, and they'd take it back. They'd come to my house, knocking on the door, "Excuse me, we meant to give that to someone else. That was going to Meryl Streep."'*

## 'When I won the Oscar, I thought it was a fluke'

Most people who experience the impostor syndrome are unaware how many people feel the same way. It is like watching a swan glide over the water, you are not aware of how much churn is going on underneath. We tend to notice other people as confident swans rather than seeing the internal angst they may be experiencing.

A sure way to have low self-esteem and make yourself feel inferior is to compare what you see in others on the outside, with what you are experiencing yourself on the inside. You will always come off worse.

**What Can Be Done About It?**

The first step in addressing your thoughts of doubt, uncertainty and low self-worth in a situation is to recognize it could well be the imposter syndrome at work and know that you are not alone.

The following exercise is also very useful to manage the thought process that is creating your belief that you are flying by the seat of your pants, out of your depth and about to get found out as a fraud. It is based on this simple question...

## What Do You Say When You Talk To Yourself?

It's a strange question and yet it is the most significant factor in determining how you are going to think about a situation, which will affect how you then feel and act. Confident people talk to themselves differently to people who are full of self-doubt. As Henry Ford, founder of the Ford motor company, put it, *"Whether you think you can, or think you can't... you're right."*

What you say when you talk to yourself is about being aware of what you focus on and what you are telling yourself *is* going to happen.

There is a part of you (you can think of it like a character inside your head) that is positive and likely to help you to get you through challenging situations; and another part (again, think of a character inside your head that represents this part) that will undermine your success in the same situation.

The skill that successful people develop is in being able to tune in to the part that will help when they need it most and the following exercise can help you to challenge your self-limiting beliefs by identifying what they are and then tuning in to a more useful thought or internal voice.

17

## Exercise: Challenging Self-limiting Beliefs

Grab a sheet of paper and draw a line down the centre.

**Step 1:** Think of something that takes you out of your comfort zone and makes you feel unconfident or anxious. In the left hand column, write a list of what you are saying, specifically, the words you are telling yourself, about this situation. Really tune in to the voice and let the comments flow as you get them down on paper. Eg. "I'm going to forget my words" or "It will be awful like last time!"

When you have written down your specific thoughts, take a moment to read through them and notice how it makes you feel. Take a deep breath and move on to Step 2...

**Step 2:** For each thought you have written on the left hand side, you are now going to think of a counter thought to this – a thought that is *equally true* – that comes from a more nurturing part of you.

This is the voice that you have probably developed based on people in your life who have supported, encouraged and rallied for you. The part that feels more confident and able to deal with situations.

For each thought on the left-hand side find a counter thought until you have filled out the right-hand column. Take a moment to read through them and notice how it makes you feel.

**Step 3:** Now cross out the thoughts in column 1 so only column 2 on the right is readable. This is where you need to focus your thinking when you think about this situation. Each time from now, you catch yourself back on the left-hand side with a negative thought, remind yourself of the counter thought on the left-hand side.

What we focus on becomes our reality. The more you practice focusing your thoughts on the right-hand side, the easier it will be to access a confident state of mind about a situation.

As Mohammed Ali put it... "I am the greatest, I said that even before I was". What you say to yourself about a situation will become a self-fulfilling prophecy.

## "I am the greatest, I said that even before I was"

## The Victim Trap

Another way to focus your thinking to feel more confident is to become aware of the Victim Trap.

When I am coaching, I can usually spot very quickly when a client is in the Victim Trap. The clues are in the way they describe events, the low level of personal influence they believe they have in managing situations and the degree of blame they apportion to other people.

We have the power to step out of the Victim Trap by managing our thinking, so rather than perceiving events and people or situations as outside of our control or feeling overwhelmed, we can take back control by focusing on what we *can* influence.

Steven Covey in his book 'The 7 Habits of Highly Effective People' identified that, in any given situation, you can have one of three types of control:

**1. Direct Control** – the power to change or influence a situation is directly within your control

**2. Indirect Control** – other people will also be involved who you need to influence to make changes happen

**3. No Control** – situations where our only control is in our response to the situation

You can influence your personal outcome in each of these types of situation by determining where you focus your attention and how your self-talk affects your perspective.

Confidence is about feeling in control - if not of people and events, then at least feeling in control of your own response or actions.  By stepping out of the Victim Trap and taking charge of your life, being responsible for it, rather than blaming events or situations that happen to you, you will feel more empowered, which feeds your confidence.

Confident people are good at focusing on where they have influence to change things – taking the tiller and steering the boat rather than feeling like they are bobbing on the ocean at the mercy of the winds and currents.

# Exercise: Your Locus Of Control

Grab a piece of paper and draw a large circle, with two smaller circles inside, a bit like a bullseye. Label the centre circle 'Direct Control', the next circle out 'Indirect Control' and the outside circle 'No Control'. This is your Locus of Control 'map'.

**Step 1:** Make a list of things that are concerns to you at this moment in time – from major events that are preying on your mind, right down to small issues that affect you.

**Step 2:** Go down the list and plot them somewhere on your Locus of Control map. Decide which circle they fall into.

**Step 3:** Having decided what kind of control you have, decide what you want to do about each item on your map. In your area of:

**Direct Control** in the centre – what action can you take to improve things;

**Indirect Control** – who else is involved, how can you influence or collaborate with them:

**No Control** – how can you change your attitude to this? What actions can you take to make things better despite not being able to change what has happened?

**Step 4:** Decide when and how you are going to act, and write your actions (either next to each point on your map or you may create a list next to the map).

Your confidence will grow when you practice shifting focus from a victim state (where things are happening to you); to a creative state (where you cause things to happen, directly or indirectly).

Fundamentally, we often can't control events, or other people's actions, but we can control how we react to them.  When you decide you have 'no control' in a situation, you can choose instead to focus on your response-ability...

## How Response-able Are You?

Response-ability is a measure of how you can manage your reaction to events, by understanding how your feelings are fuelled by your beliefs.  If you can learn to pause before you react, you can readjust your perspective by challenging your thinking about it.

Pausing to reflect is one of the key practices of the ancient wisdom of Stoicism.

Stoics believe it is not what happens to us that causes distress, but the meaning we give to what happens to us. Events don't upset you, beliefs do.

Rather than being driven by your beliefs of what is 'right and wrong', you can learn to take a negative outlook (based on angry thoughts/beliefs) and turn it into a more peaceful perspective on life by having calmer thoughts about a situation. The stoic view is that getting angry about things (particularly those we have no control over) is futile and can become self-destructive.

## 'Events don't upset you, beliefs do.'

The skill lies in developing **your ability to pause**, and notice what you are thinking about something before you choose your response or decide what this means to you. Where you may have an initial thought about something, pausing to reflect on the wider context of this situation can really help to 'put it into perspective' – particularly if that perspective makes things seem better.

So, in any given situation, rather than thinking about how bad this is; you can challenge your perspective by considering what other scenarios could be happening that would be a lot worse.

This then has the effect of making you realize the current situation isn't so bad after all.

*For example, imagine you are in a queue in a supermarket and the other queues are all moving. It is clear you have picked the 'wrong' queue to get in and this creates feelings of frustration, irritation and impatience.*

*To shift your perspective, focus on how things could be worse than this – ranging from what could be mildly worse (for example, you could also have a headache) right through to major disasters (for example, you could have lost your livelihood and no longer afford to buy this food) to life-threatening scenarios (a machine-gun toting maniac could run in and kill us all).*

*Given these other possibilities, and your good luck that none of these worse scenarios are happening, the comparative reality of having to wait 5 minutes extra in this queue is really not worth worrying about.*

Once you can master the ability to pause and readjust your perspective, you have greater power over your thoughts and beliefs, which promotes a calmer, less reactive, state.

As the expression goes, 'Don't Sweat The Small Stuff (And It's All Small Stuff)"

# Exercise: The Stoic Pause

Consider the following situations, and identify what you could focus on to reassess your current reality in a comparatively better light:

**Example:**
*Situation*: Stuck in a supermarket queue when you are in a hurry:

*Could be worse scenarios*: I could... not have the money to shop here, feel unwell, have nowhere to sleep tonight, find out someone I love has been mugged outside, have six months to live.

Think about how you might shift your focus on these:

*Situation*: Somebody else gets the recognition award you were expecting to win.

*What 'could be worse' scenarios* can you think of?


*Situation*: Somebody goes up the outside and cuts in front of you in a long traffic jam.

*What 'could be worse' scenarios* can you think of?

*Situation*: Having to work late and missing an evening out

*What 'could be worse' scenarios* can you think of?


What other situations do you find frustrating? (you may want to write down a few)

*What 'could be worse' scenarios* can you think of?

Getting into the habit of mastering your thoughts, by focusing on "could be worse, I could..." takes practice, but if you can learn to refocus your thinking, you will find it creates a more positive perspective on events, which in the long run gives you far greater confidence in yourself to manage your peace of mind.

As Epictetus put it,

*"Remember...if someone succeeds in provoking you, realize that your mind is complicit in the provocation. Which is why it is essential that we not respond impulsively to impressions; take a moment before reacting, and you will find it is easier to maintain control."*

**Epictetus - Enchiridion XX**

# Chapter 3:

# MANAGING YOUR EMOTIONS

# "No one can make you feel inferior without your consent"

Eleanor Roosevelt

# Chapter 3: Managing Your Emotions

Our emotions are key to our self-confidence.
Following the TEA model, negative emotions will
cause us to have negative thoughts and take
actions we may later regret; just as positive
emotions will have the reverse effect.

*It was the end of a long, tiring week, when Sarah
Jones boarded the 18.12 train at Waterloo. Her
feet were stinging in her tight-fitting shoes, her
head was starting to throb, and her stomach
quietly rumbled as a reminder that she hadn't
eaten for several hours.*

*She was mildly comforted at the thought of the
packet of biscuits she had found time to buy at
the station shop so at least she could ease her
hunger, if not her aching feet and head.*

*She found her seat and closed her eyes as the
train slowly juddered into motion. On opening
her eyes, she was aware of the dishevelled youth
sitting across from her, with his three-day
stubble, his mean-looking tattoo across his
forehead and his studded jacket that gave off a
faint smell of stale patchouli.*

*Too weary and hungry to think any further, she
opened the packet of biscuits and savoured the
sugary taste as she contentedly munched away.*

*Suddenly, the teenager reached over, grabbed the packet off the table and helped himself. His eyes met Sarah's as if to challenge her to say something.*

*She couldn't believe his nerve but, feeling reluctant to cause a scene, said nothing. Instead, she picked up the packet, and glaring across at him, took another biscuit.*

*Once again, he picked up the biscuits and helped himself. He even smiled at her as he loudly chomped away on his biscuit without any sense of discomfort or shame.*

*By now, she felt incensed by his rudeness, but didn't want to speak up and tell him what she thought of him.*

*Watching him sit there munching away, defiantly challenging her to respond, she felt so angry, it was as if a week's worth of frustrations at work were now being fused into this one moment of fury at his lack of respect.*

*In a peak of rage, she picked up the biscuits, shot him a filthy look and marched off to another carriage.*

*Once settled in her new seat, she opened her bag to put the biscuits away, when she found, sitting in her bag, the unopened packet of biscuits that she had bought at the station. It was his biscuits she had been eating.*

## What If I'm Wrong?

Negative emotions are often triggered by our thoughts and beliefs - as in this story about the biscuits - and can cause us to act in a way we regret, or fuel further negative thoughts, which undermine our confidence.

If we can manage our emotions, take responsibility for our own feelings rather than allow other events, people or thoughts to affect our self-confidence and inner calm, we will enjoy far greater wellbeing.

The problem is that so often we are pulled off-balance because we do not pay attention to what we are feeling and why we are feeling that way. We feel powerless to change our feelings, rather than identifying what thoughts, beliefs and behaviours are *causing us* to feel this way,

The Quakers have a saying "*and what if I'm wrong?*" as a useful counter-balance to becoming too attached to a particular belief, opinion or dogma. It is a useful question to consider, particularly if you want to feel more in control of your thought-led emotions.

# **Exercise:** Emotional Check-In

The following questions are useful to ask yourself to start to notice what is behind your emotions when you don't feel confident:

1. How am I feeling?

2. What is causing me to feel like this?
What thoughts and beliefs am I aware of that are contributing to my mood?

3. How would I rather feel?

4. What would help me to feel like this?

What can I think about to shift my emotional state?

What behaviour would help me to shift my emotional state?

5. What can I do right now to feel better?

## Mastering Your Emotions

Nelson Mandela is a good example of someone who learned early on in his struggle that he needed to master his emotions as his fiery impulses caused him to do and say things he would regret afterwards.

According to the author Richard Stengel, who collaborated with Mandela on his autobiography 'Long Walk to Freedom', when Mandela entered prison he was "not in control of his emotions. The man who came out was in very rigorous control of his passions and his emotions." He still felt things deeply, but he had learned that he needed to control his emotions to achieve his aims.

## Having Greater Emotional Control

Being able to control your emotional response to situations rather than responding in a 'mindless', knee-jerk way, is something that takes practice, but gets easier the more you do it. Similar to the Stoic Pause of the previous chapter, where you use a pause to question your thinking, the key to staying emotionally calm is being able to pause to choose your response.

The trick is to practice when you are not as emotionally triggered by something so that you have got better at pausing when something really hits your 'hot buttons'.

Whenever you are have a powerful emotional reaction, immediately take a deep breath and separate the event from your impression of it. The event is what happened; your "impression" is how you have, initially, instinctively viewed it.

So how can you enhance your emotional response-ability? What will help you to manage to pause before feeling negatively about something?

## Exercise: Mind The Gap

Grab a piece of paper (or use the pages at the back of the book to write on)

**Step 1:** Write a list of the situations where you most need to pause (but find it hard) and also situations where you would find it relatively easy to pause before responding (even if you don't currently pause at these times).

Grade each situation between 1-10 in 'pause difficulty' (with 1 being so easy it almost wouldn't count and 10 being virtually impossible).

**Step 2:** Think of all the things that could help you to pause before responding (eg. Counting to 10 in your head...or maybe 5!, squeezing your toes to the floor, breathing in and out 3 times, ...and add your own ideas)

**Step 3:** Plan to start: put a star by situations you can do in the next 24 hours that are below a 5 on your list.  Then over the next week, once you have some practice under your belt, have a go at one of the higher pause challenges.

Try out different ideas until you find the method of pausing that suits you best and keep practicing until it becomes second nature when you get 'triggered' to be able to pause.

## State Anchoring

Another useful tool to help you access a more useful emotional state to the one you are experiencing is called state 'anchoring'.

Ivan Pavlov, the Russian physiologist, first discovered the idea of stimulus response in the 19th Century.  He noticed that if he rang a bell when he fed his dog and repeated this a number of times, he got the point where the dog would salivate if the bell rang, even if there was no food.

The dog had become conditioned to react automatically to the stimulus.

The idea of stimulus-response works equally with your own emotions and the process called 'anchoring' allows you to create a desired state by forming a neural pathway in your mind which links a stimulus to a response you want to experience.

We experience anchors all the time – the teacher asks a question and we put our hand up if we think we have the answer, we see a red traffic light and we stop our car then automatically move forward again when the light changes. We might smell freshly cut grass and emotionally feel positive that spring is here – or we might feel negatively as it reminds of a time when we were taking end of school exams and feeling stressed.

The following exercise will help you to use anchoring to create your personal 'Ring of Confidence'. The more you practice this, the more powerful it will be in helping you access a confident state when you need it. Read through the exercise first, so you know how to do it and then try it out (or get someone else to read it out as you go through the exercise).

# Exercise: Your Ring of Confidence

**Step1**: Imagine you have a ring of confidence like a spotlight on the floor, which you can step into at any time... When you step into this ring you can access the feeling of confidence

**Step 2**: Take a moment to identify a time when you most intensely experienced feeling really confident

Step into your imaginary 'ring' and close your eyes to help you recreate the experience, as though you were there again:

Notice what you **See** (people, objects, background scenery, colours), what you **Hear** (sounds, internal and external voices, silence) and what you **Feel** (emotions, sensations, locations, strengths.) Allow these feelings to grow and intensify as you reconnect with the experience of confidence

**Step 3**: Break your concentration by opening your eyes, stepping back out of the ring and bringing your attention back to the room

**Step 4**: Repeat the process a second time by stepping back into the ring and repeat **Step 2** to relive your confident experience.

**Step 5:** Step back out, open your eyes and bring your attention back to the room again.

**Step 6:** Pick up your ring – throw it down in a different spot and repeat the experience of **Step 2**, knowing that you can return to this experience of confidence, and enjoy these feelings, whenever you step into your Confidence Ring.

## Building Up Emotional Resilience

Emotional resilience – which you can build-up by continually investing in feeling well as a daily practice - provides another useful foundation for Emotional Mastery.

This kind of emotional self-renewal makes it far easier to weather the knocks to your mood or confidence, because if you are starting from a point of feeling well, you are likely to be more emotionally resilient to manage whatever happens to you each day.

## Quick-fix Mood Enhancers

It is useful to reflect on *your* personal mood enhancers – those quick fix adjustments that can help you shift your emotional state to feel better,

**so you can be mindful to experience them more frequently by planning them into your week.**

Here is a list to get you started... what would you add to the list as the kind of 'fix' that tends to make you feel better?

- Exercise – sport – playing games

- Music – playing or listening

- Contacting/Phoning/meeting up with a friend

- Helping someone out – volunteering

- Gratitude – keeping a journal of what you are grateful for – thanking people – noticing what is positive about your situation or life

- Watch a funny film/TV/live show

- Dance – Zumba – Tai Chi – Private disco in your kitchen with the music turned up

- Spending time with animals or nature

- Meditating – relaxing

- Planning a future event you are excited about

- Setting goals you feel energized to achieve

- Enjoying a spiritual moment (religious or otherwise)

- Curl up by a fire with a good read and warm drink

- Focusing on the people who make your life better/ you are glad to know

- Enjoying an absorbing hobby

- **What else would you add in the space below that lifts your mood??**

**Your Personal Confidence Bank**

In this chapter we have focused on how you can have greater influence on your emotional state and resilience.

This final exercise will give you a further resource to draw from when you want to feel more confident, by having your own 'bank' of positive memories that you can draw on when you need to remind yourself of what confidence feels like for you.

# Exercise: Your Confidence Bank

Grab a piece of paper and write a line down the middle of the page.

**Step 1:** On the left-hand side put the heading **'When Do I Feel More Confident**?' and create a list of the situations or times in your life when you feel confident about yourself, your skills and talents, your achievements. Add to your list significant 'highlights' from your past, warm moments and memories and any positive feedback from others – however small – plus all those times when you felt positive or confident about things.

**Step 2:** On the right-hand side put the heading 'What created this feeling?' and notice for each situation or experience in the left column, what contributed to this feeling of emotional wellbeing. Include the places, people, what you were doing, the environment... everything that was significant to you feeling this way.

**Step 3:** Notice what common themes come up when you are feeling good. Are there any features that you could be incorporating into your day-to-day experience more often?

# Chapter 4:

# CONFIDENT BEHAVIOUR

# "Feel the fear and do it anyway"

## Susan Jeffers

# Chapter 4: Confident Behaviour

The third area of the TEA model is about how we can impact our thoughts and emotions by managing our Actions.

**Confident Body Language**

In her excellent TED talk 'Your Body Language May Shape Who You Are', Amy Cuddy, a professor of social psychology at Harvard, introduces the idea of specific 'power poses' which can influence other people and even your own brain.

Prof Cuddy and her research team conducted an experiment in which a group of people were interviewed for a job. Half the group were left to sit in reception while waiting to go into the interview and the other half were given a specific 'power pose' called the Superman or Wonder Woman pose.

After the interviews, the interviewers were asked which people they would be likely to offer a job. Without exception it was the group who had adopted the power pose. The interviewers' comments included remarks like... "as soon as they walked in, they had something about them".

This kind of experiment has been conducted in various forms for many years and each time what we learn is that we can communicate confidence non-verbally through our body language – even when we don't necessarily feel or think confidently initially, our confidence can be led by our actions or behaviour.

## Exercise: Adopting The Superman or Wonder Woman Pose

Try it now. To adopt the pose, stand with your feet about hip width apart, and clench your fists into balls and put them on your waist at either side – as Superman or Wonder Woman would stand, looking ahead, with your back straight.

Stand like this for 2 minutes and notice how it affects your confidence.

### Aligning Your Verbal And Non-verbal Message

Your body language will not only affect your self-confidence, it also communicates confidence to other people more than you may realise as most people can tell by looking at us how we are feeling and what we are thinking.

'Fake it till you make it' does work when it comes to boosting your confidence through body language. If you want to feel better, simply adopting confident posture will help. Conversely, if people feel depressed their body language automatically mirrors and reinforces their low mood.

Here are a few basic ideas that with practice will help you to appear more confident, until your feelings and thoughts have caught up.

1. Posture: Standing up straight conveys confidence. If you keep your shoulders slightly back with your chin slightly up, standing symmetrically, it helps give you a confident posture. Try it in front of the mirror and just notice the difference.

2. Eyes – try to look people in the eye when you speak to them – not in an intense way, but enough that it doesn't look like you are avoiding eye contact, which can start your self-talk, undermining your confidence.

3. Hands – try to keep them still, apart from when you are specifically gesturing, as fidgeting with your hands, wildly gesticulating or hiding your hands all conveys a lack of confidence.

4. Firm handshake – not floppy or crushing but keep your grip firm (not tight) and combine it with eye contact and a smile. Confident people smile because they are feeling ok. Again, fake it till you make it.

5. Move with confidence – keep your posture upright and move with intention, rather than shuffling – while keeping your facial expression warm.

There is something called the 'comfort zone paradox' which is that what looks right feels wrong – at least initially – but what may feel uncomfortable when you first try it will get easier with practice.

**Breathing Confidence**

Breathing is a massive factor in feeling and sounding confident. Not only does your breath affect your voice and how confident you sound, it can also help you to manage your adrenaline in situations where your confidence is shaky and you start to feel anxious.

When we feel unconfident or anxious, adrenaline is released into our blood stream, our thoughts become panicky and our breathing becomes more shallow, from our chest, and much quicker to match our increased heart rate.

Even if you were feeling calm and relaxed, you would be able to create a sense of fear and anxiety by mimicking this kind of breathing, while focusing on a scary thought.

Just as you can simulate anxiety through breathing, so can you calm your fear and anxiety by managing how you breath and where you focus your attention.

## Exercise: Confident Breathing Technique

Step 1: Correct your posture so you are standing tall and shake out any tension in your body. Shake again until you have relaxed your muscles and do an exaggerated yawn to relax your face.

Step 2: Put one hand on your belly and breathe in through your nose so deeply that you push your hand out with your belly. Hold for a few seconds and then blow out through your mouth as if you were slowly putting out several candles on a cake.

**Step 3:** Breathe normally as you give your body another good shake – your arms, legs and wiggle your shoulders. Roll your neck to release any tension and have another yawn.

**Step 4:** Take another deep breath down to your belly and as you do so, think of someone you really care about, who also cares about you and as you hold their image in your mind, breathe out this time more slowly and calmly.

**Repeat Step 4** as many times as you want to until you feel calm and connected with the thought of how much this person enriches your life.

## Mental Rehearsal

A final exercise to use Actions to promote your confidence is Mental Rehearsal. By Mentally Rehearsing – playing through in our mind how you want things to go - you are creating an experience of what you want to happen, rather than what you don't want to happen.

When we are apprehensive about something, we naturally 'mentally rehearse' - except In our minds we see ourselves in the middle of what we don't want to happen. The following mental rehearsal technique allows you to imagine things going well instead.

# Exercise: Mentally Rehearsing Confidence

**Step 1:** Think of a situation where you would like to be more confident. Identify specifically when and where is would be most useful and appropriate to be more confident.

**Step 2:** Close your eyes and in your mind, imagine you are watching a film of yourself in this situation as an observer (as if you were in a cinema watching the film on the screen). Start the film and notice yourself performing your part in the situation. Notice who else is with you and what is being said. Allow the performance to finish and then take the film back to the start.

**Step 3:** Watch the film again, this time making whatever adjustments or improvements you would like to your confidence and behaviour to create the best possible version of this situation. Notice the different responses of other people each time you improve your confident performance.

You can rewind and replay the film as many times as you need to in order to produce the most excellent performance of confidence that you can.

**Step 4:** Now that you have created a film of the most excellent performance possible, imagine you replay it again, but this time you are going to step into the film as if you are actually in it, looking through your own eyes, noticing what you can hear, what you are saying to yourself, and become aware of what it feels like to behave like this, feeling this confident.

**Step 5:** You can keep rewinding and replaying the film, as if you are in it, making whatever adjustments - to your posture, gestures, tone of voice or your choice of words - will improve your confident performance even more.

Repeat this process until you have the best version of this performance – as you would like it to be.

Just notice how it feels when you can enjoy feeling this confident in this situation.

**Step 6:** Finally, become aware of situations and events coming up when you want to behave like this.


## "Imagination is everything... it is the preview of life's coming attractions"

**Albert Einstein**

# Chapter 5:

# HOW TO BE MORE ASSERTIVE

**"The meek do not inherit the Earth, they serve those who are self-confident and self assertive."**

Dean Koontz

# Chapter 5: How To Be More Assertive

Some people are **aggressive**. Hell-bent on winning, they believe their needs matter most. They are controlling, tend to lack respect for other people and will often have a complete disregard for the needs, feelings and opinions of others. Their communication style can be angry, domineering, self-centred and manipulative. You probably know people who behave like this.

Some people are **passive**. Submissive to the needs of others, they are afraid that if they speak up they may offend people or make them angry. They do not regard themselves as equals because they place greater importance on the rights, wishes and feelings of others. Their needs get ignored. You probably know people like this too.

Then there are those people who recognise the importance of meeting their needs AND other people's needs in equal measure. They tend to have strong self-esteem, positive self-talk, feel capable to communicate well to identify what will be agreeable to people and have positive experiences of win/win conversations so that everyone leaves feeling ok. They are **assertive.**

While we may all act in aggressive, passive and assertive ways at times, depending on the context – who else is involved and what is at stake – the ability to communicate assertively tends to be closely linked to self-confidence and self-esteem, based on a mindset of 'I'm OK, You're OK'.

As with many of the ideas we have covered in this book, assertive behaviour is habit-forming, takes practice, but is a skill that will reap many benefits for you and your confidence in dealing with other people.

Aggressive and Passive behaviour is often a result of your upbringing and life influences and can also be a symptom of low self-esteem. The problem is that being unassertive frequently leaves an aftertaste of guilt, regret and frustration, not to mention the damage it can do to your relationships and your confidence.

Unassertive behaviour is usually developed early in life and can be a vicious cycle. If your family taught you to place the needs of others before yourself as a child, it may be difficult for you to assert yourself. Equally, if your family handled conflict by yelling and arguing, you may have learned to deal with conflict accordingly.

The point is that whatever has been your habitual communication style, or your life experiences to date, anyone can learn to adopt a more assertive mindset and behaviour, to achieve win/win outcomes that meet your needs **and** other people's.

**Assertiveness And The TEA Model**

Assertive behaviour is characterised by the following Thoughts, Emotions and Actions:

**Thoughts:** Assertive people focus on win/win thinking, by actively seeking to empathise and understand another person's point of view with respect and curiosity, asking questions to gain greater insight into other people's needs, and trying to find workable solutions that are mutually agreeable.

**Emotions:** Assertive people manage to stay calm, so they can express their needs and listen to other's needs without with getting emotional or feeling frustrated. They have learnt how to manage their impulsive responses and knee-jerk emotional 'outbursts'.

**Actions:** Assertive people align their body language (eyes, posture, voice, breathing) to their words.  They also tend to walk their talk with their actions so build trust in what they say.  They behave with respect for themselves and others.

## Basic Principles Of Assertiveness

The fundamental principles of assertiveness is that you have:

- Self-care & respect for others
- A Win-win mindset
- Adult to adult communication
- Courage & Consideration in having your and others' needs met

# Exercise: Assertiveness & You

Grab a piece of paper and write your answers to these questions:

1. In what kind of situations would you like to be more assertive?

2. What is your usual style of communication?

3. What stops you being assertive?  What is your greatest challenge to assertive behaviour?

4. What is the pay-off for being more assertive?

## Assertiveness Communication Tools

To become more assertive in your communication, it is useful to have some tools at your disposal that will help you to communicate your needs while considering other people's needs.

## 1. Broken Record

This first technique is very useful when you want to assert your needs without entering into arguments or having to justify your reasons for your needs.

Broken Record works by using calm repetition to reinforce your message as a phrase that helps you to help you stick to your desired point without being swung by someone else's manipulation or counter-arguments.  You can use additional phrases to acknowledge what others have said to you, but your response always includes your 'broken record' phrase.

It is a classic assertiveness technique, but one that should be used with caution, as it can break rapport with the other person if it becomes too robotic.  Also, it risks being too focused on your needs, without taking into account the other person's needs.

The power of the Broken Record technique is that it creates a consistent message and eventually people will give up trying to convince you of alternatives to your desired outcome.

For example, if you took something back to a shop and wanted a refund, your broken record phrase would be "I would like a refund." If the sales assistant was giving you reasons that the goods were adequate or no longer stocked or any other reasons they didn't want to take them back, you would assert "I understand they are adequate/no longer in stock/whatever other reason they have given... and 'I would like a refund'.  Without engaging with their reasons, you calmly repeat your needs.

# Exercise: Broken Record

Think about when this would be useful to you. In what situations could you use the Broken Record technique?

What phrase would you repeat?

How might other people respond to you?

How would you word a response to this that acknowledges what they have said, while still repeating your phrase?

## 2. Workable Compromise – Saying "No" Nicely

Workable Compromise is useful when it is important to stay in rapport with someone, by being able to say 'no' to their request without causing offence or risk falling out.

The technique works by acknowledging the other person's position first, then asserting your point, before suggesting an option that takes both positions into account.

There are three phrases you use to acknowledge the relative needs of both parties, as follows:

**"I understand**.... (the other person's need)
**"But I**....(your need)"
**"So What if**.... (a solution that addresses both needs)

For example, if someone asked you to work late but you had a prior social arrangement, you might say:

*"I understand you want me to work late, But I have arranged to meet someone at 6pm, So what if I come in early to spend some time on it then?"*

## **Exercise:** Workable Compromise

When might you use Workable Compromise?

In what situations would it be most useful?

Consider how you would complete the sentences in those situations:

"I Understand ...

"But I ...

"So what if ...

## 3. Creating An Assertive 'Bubble'

Most people respond negatively to criticism and this is one of the greater barriers to assertive communication.

The ability to receive a critical comment or perceived criticism without automatically hitting back with a negative remark (or retreating hurt), has a massive impact on assertiveness.

An Assertive 'Bubble' is very useful as an idea to help with this. The idea is that you imagine you are immersing yourself in a protective bubble, which doesn't allow criticism to penetrate - and cause you to react emotionally - when you want to stay calm to be assertive.

When people criticize us, it is easy to react to the criticism rather than calmly consider what they have said, while being curious about what has prompted them to say it.

While you are in the calm space of your Assertive Bubble, you can acknowledge there may be some truth in someone's criticism of you with getting emotional, as you ask for more information about what has caused the person to comment.

This gives you a greater sense of control plus the time to consider what they have said and how you can assertively respond to it.

There are 3 parts to your response:

1. Acknowledge the behaviour they have commented on
2. Stay Calm
3. Ask for more information

For example, if someone accuses you of making a stupid mistake, from the calm of your Assertive Bubble, you might say:

"I agree that it was a mistake (acknowledge the criticism), but I wouldn't say it was 'stupid (staying calm).  What makes you think it was stupid (negative enquiry)?"

or if someone says "you're lazy!", you could say:

"Yes, I can be lazy (acknowledge). What is in particular you think I have been lazy about? (staying calm & negative enquiry).

It is important to follow your response with a pause while you listen from your Assertive Bubble.

## Exercise: Listening From Your Bubble

When do you tend to react emotionally, when it would be more useful to enter your Assertive Bubble? (ie. In which situations? With what kind of people?)


What kind of critical remarks might trigger you to react emotionally?


What would help you remember to get in and stay in your bubble for the conversation?


What kind of response could you use in these situations to acknowledge the behaviour they have commented on and ask for more information?

## 4. Speaking As An Adult

Transactional Analysis (TA) is useful to understand what can create barriers to assertive communication and behaviour.

TA was developed by the psychologist Eric Berne, who identified three ego states that affect our behaviour: Parent, Adult, Child.

Our **Parent** state is the voice of authority – which can manifest as a 'Critical Parent' or 'Nurturing Parent' based on the beliefs we have been taught, behaviours we have learnt and the context of the situation.

Our **Adult** state is how we think and communicate without getting emotional, based on the facts that we are dealing with – this represents our logical mind.

We enter our **Child** state when we become emotional, creative or playful – which can either be as a 'Rebellious Child' or a 'Playful Child'. This state represents our raw emotions, our 'unadulterated' responses.

When we enter into a communication with others we will do so from one of these ego states and so will they.

There are several dynamics that can happen as our ego state interacts with another person's ego state, which can result in us unintentionally behaving in a non-assertive way.

The significance of these ego states when it comes to being assertive is that it is very easy for us to be 'triggered' by someone who is not communicating from an adult ego state.

If they are in a Parent State, it can force us to react in a Child State and become overly emotional or passive.

If they are in a Child State, it can force us to become judgmental or aggressive.

By understanding the dynamics of TA, we can be aware of when we are no longer in an Adult state and make a conscious choice to get back to that State by focusing on the facts, rather than making judgments, becoming critical or getting emotional about the situation.

# Exercise: Speaking As An Adult

Think of a situation where you are likely to be triggered into a non-Adult ego state.

What will help you to return to an Adult State, when you enter a Parent State (and become judgmental or critical) or a Child State (and become emotional or disruptive)?

How can this awareness help you to be more assertive when communicating with others?

# Chapter 6:

# NEXT STEPS

**"You are what you do, not what you say you'll do"**

Carl Jung

# Chapter 6: Next Steps

So, having understood the theory of how you can become more self-confident and assertive, the big issue is what are you going to actually DO about it?

## Exercise: Action Stations

Take a moment to think about your answers to the following questions:

1. Where, when and with whom do you want to be more confident?

2. What specifically are you going to do as a result of the ideas in this book to improve?

3. What is the first action you will take?

4. What could stop you doing this and how can you make it very likely to happen?

5. How will you find further opportunities to practice these skills?

6. How will you recover if you return to your old, familiar ways?

7. What are you going to do straightaway? On closing this book?

## One-Day Workshops and Coaching Support

We hope you have found this book useful. To find out more about how we can help with personal coaching or training workshops, please get in touch with us by phone or email:

**The Communication Works**
**The Innovation Centre**
**Daresbury**
**Cheshire**
**WA4 4FS**

**Tel: (UK) 01925 393155**
**contact@hopkinsandball.com**

# Notes

# Notes

# Notes

# Notes